BY ANN DUGAN AND THE EDITORS OF
CONSUMER GUIDE®

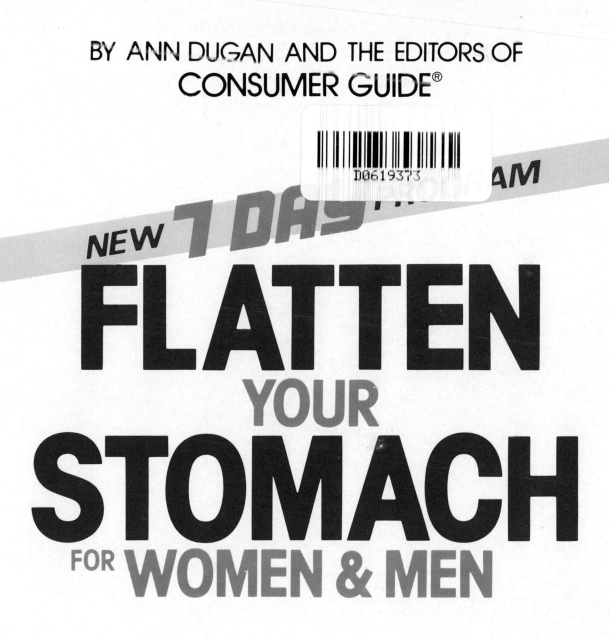

NEW 7 DAY PROGRAM

FLATTEN
YOUR
STOMACH
FOR WOMEN & MEN

BEEKMAN HOUSE
New York

Louis Weber, President
Publications International, Ltd.
3841 West Oakton Street
Skokie, Illinois 60076

Permission is never granted for commercial purposes.

Manufactured in the United States of America
10 9 8 7 6 5 4

Library of Congress Catalog Card Number: 83-60519
ISBN: 0-517-40837-6

This edition published by:
Beekman House
Distributed by Crown Publishers, Inc.
One Park Avenue
New York, New York 10016

Photography: Sam Griffith Studios, Inc.
Cover Design: Frank E. Peiler
Book Design: Ingeborg Jakobson

Contents

The 7 Day Program

Everyone wants a flat stomach. We all want the attractive, fit, youthful look of a narrow waist, a firm abdomen. Of course, paying attention to what you eat is essential to your health and fitness. But weight loss alone will not give you the firm, flat stomach you want. What really gives a body a terrific shape is well-toned muscles.

Proper exercise can shape up any stomach, no matter how far gone. But you need a regular, carefully planned exercise program. You need a program that tones all the muscles in the abdomen. There are four major abdominal muscles. Some of these muscles run up and down. Others run side to side. Some crisscross the abdomen at an angle. If you exercise only one of these muscles (say, by doing only sit-ups), your stomach may be hard. But it won't be flat.

The New 7 Day Program to Flatten Your Stomach works by evenly toning all of the abdomen's muscles. It is designed to meet the special fitness needs of both women and men. This simple, easy-to-follow program will flatten your stomach, trim your waistline, firm your midriff.

The Flatten Your Stomach program gives you an exercise plan for every day of the week. Each exercise routine takes only about 30 minutes. The exercises are foolproof and easy to follow. The entire program has been designed to produce balanced muscle development and shaping, while avoiding injury and soreness. Follow this simple program, exercising regularly and vigorously each day. You'll feel more fit, energetic, self-confident, and attractive in just a few short weeks.

Following the program

The new Flatten Your Stomach program offers 7 new exercise routines—a different routine for every day of the week. During the first 6 days, the program alternates days of lighter exercise with days of more vigorous exercise, as recommended by medical experts on physical fitness. At the same time, the exercises gradually progress from Day 1 on, so that Day 6 is the most vigorous—and most beneficial—routine of the week. Day 7 is a maintenance-level routine. You might want to arrange your weekly exercise program so that you do the Day 7 routine when you may have less time or energy to devote to exercise, perhaps on the weekend.

Each of the 7 new routines includes warm-up exercises, spot exercises to flatten the stomach, stretches for flexibility, and cool-down exercises. Most fitness experts agree that each type of exercise serves an important purpose. Each is essential to a sound fitness program.

Warm ups get your body going. They generally loosen up the muscles all over your body and get your heart and lungs working at higher levels. Warm ups are essential for two main reasons.

When your body is properly warmed up, the more vigorous stomach exercises will be more effective. Warm ups raise the body and muscle temperature to efficient levels. They increase the blood supply in the muscles and increase the rate and force of muscle contractions. Your car works more efficiently after the engine is properly warmed up. The same is true for your body.

Warm ups also make you less prone to injury when you go on to more vigorous exercises. They stretch the ligaments and tissues to permit greater flexibility. By gradually activating muscle fibers, you'll help prevent muscle tears and sprains. How will you know when you've warmed up enough? You'll be slightly out of breath, and you'll break the sweat barrier.

The exercises for the stomach are a combination of spot exercises and stretches. Our *spot exercises* are muscle-toners, not ''spot reducers.'' Exercising one area of the body will not reduce the amount of fat in that area. However, our spot exercises can change the shape of an area. Restoring muscle tone makes the abdomen firmer and more attractively shaped.

Stretches are often included as the last step in an exercise. Stretches help avoid injury by increasing flexibility and range of movement. The connective tissues of your body are like rubber bands. If not stretched frequently, the tissues become tight and limit your movement. If not stretched at all for a long time, the tissues may snap, causing injury and pain. Take the stretches slowly at first. Do not stretch any farther than you feel comfortable. As the ligaments gradually loosen, your stretches will go farther.

The stomach-flattening exercises are carefully designed to help your muscles develop evenly. This even development of all the abdomen's different muscles is what gives you the shape and proportion you're after. Our exercise routines carefully alternate the muscles exercised. One exercise may work on the muscles that run up and down the abdomen. The next may firm up those that run side to side. Another may work on the muscles that crisscross the abdomen. That is one more reason to do all the exercises in each routine in the order given.

Cool downs are exercises that allow your body to slow down gradually. After strenuous work, the body must readjust to pre-exercise levels of body function. Cool downs help your muscles begin to relax. They allow your circulatory system to slow down gradually. If you stop exercising suddenly, without this tapering-off period, blood collects in the muscles and veins. This could cause dizziness and weakness. A proper cool down also helps minimize stiffness and soreness.

Making it work

To get the most from the time and energy you put into this program, keep these guidelines in mind.
• Wear comfortable clothing that allows you to move freely, such as shorts, a leotard, or a light exercise suit.
• Exercise in tennis shoes, in socks, or barefoot—whatever is most comfortable

to you. If you have a weak back, weak knees, or weak ankles, wear tennis shoes or running shoes.

• If possible, exercise on a wooden floor or on a carpet. Exercising on concrete surfaces can be hard on your body. For floor exercises, try to work on a mat, a carpet remnant, a piece of foam rubber, or a folded towel.

• Try to exercise every day, or at least four times a week. A regular exercise program offers the most benefit for your body.

• Establish your own exercise schedule. You shouldn't exercise just before bedtime or just after you eat. Most any other time is fine. Once you choose the best time, stick to it. Exercising at the same time every day helps you develop the exercise habit.

• Follow the routines carefully. If you follow directions, you should tone and shape muscles properly, avoid injury, and suffer a minimum of soreness.

• If you cannot do an exercise exactly as it is described, don't worry. Try it, and then go on to the next exercise. Don't feel discouraged. As you increase your strength and flexibility, you will eventually be able to do most of the exercises. Then you will realize just how far you have progressed.

• Remember that your individual body structure may make an exercise difficult for you. Body structure and flexibility vary greatly from person to person. The structure of your joints or the length of your arms or legs may prevent you from doing an exercise exactly as it is described. Don't push yourself past your own body's limits. Aim toward what is asked for in each exercise, doing the best that you can.

• Do the number of repetitions given in the text, until the exercises are easy for you. Then gradually increase the number of repetitions for each exercise. For some exercises, the text recommends the number of repetitions you should try to work toward. In general, you might aim toward eventually doubling the repetitions given in the text. But don't try to go too far too fast. Don't try to double the repetitions all at once. Add only 3 to 5 repetitions at a time, until that number becomes easy.

• At the end of each day's exercises, you should feel a healthy, relaxed sense of fatigue. Exercise that does not tax the body does not help the body.

• No matter how rushed you may be, do not neglect to do the warm ups and cool downs. These exercises are essential for keeping your body flexible, getting your heart and lungs working efficiently, and avoiding injury and stiffness.

• As you work through each day's routine, keep your body moving. You lose some of the benefits if you take long breaks between exercises. Exercising to lively music can help you pace yourself and really keep you going.

• Learn to listen to your own body for signs of fatigue. You want to exercise vigorously enough to work up a sweat. But be careful not to overdo. If you're winded and breathless, or if you suffer sprains or stitches in the side, assume that you're exercising too vigorously. Slow down a little.

• If you haven't exercised for a while, it is

normal to be a little sore and stiff when you first start. Stiffness does not mean you should stop moving. In most cases, it means you should get going again. Remember that warming up and cooling down properly will help minimize soreness.

• If you think you may be injured, stop using the injured limb. Continuing to exercise could worsen the injury. Stop your exercise program until the injury no longer hurts when you are at rest. Then gradually begin to exercise slowly and carefully.

• To avoid back problems, always do sit-ups with the knees bent. When lifting the back off the floor or lowering the back to the floor, keep your head up, chin toward the chest. Curl the back as you lift and lower it. Also curl the back when you bend the torso over and return to an upright position.

• If you feel any tightness or discomfort in your back, take a break for a few minutes. The abdominal muscles depend on the back for much of their support. Therefore, some exercises for the abdomen may also put some strain on the back. This is especially true if your back is weak. These exercises will gradually help strengthen the back, but go slowly at first.

• If you have weak ankles or weak knees, be careful during exercises that put stress on the ankles or knees. Take it easy until you start to strengthen the muscles in those areas.

• Supplement this program with as much activity as possible. You should consciously aim at becoming a more physically active person. Try to do more walking, bicycling, dancing. Take the stairs instead of the elevator. Participate in whatever active sports you enjoy. Keep that energy level up.

• Don't be discouraged if you gain a little weight after the first week of exercise. A small weight gain means that the muscles are becoming firmer and denser. Those few extra pounds will disappear after another week of regular exercise.

• If you miss a week or more on this program, start again with the number of repetitions given in the text. You'll have to rebuild your strength and flexibility before increasing the number of repetitions again.

• All the exercises in this program were developed in consultation with medical experts. However, it is recommended that you consult your doctor before beginning this or any program of exercise.

You're on your way

Now let's get started. You have the ground rules. You understand how this terrific program works. So get into some comfortable clothes, put on some upbeat music, and get moving. It will take some effort, but it will all be worth it. Don't expect overnight results. But you'll soon notice that you're looking a little bit better every day you exercise. Within only a few weeks, this program can shape you up dramatically. The Flatten Your Stomach program will take only a few minutes each day, but the rewards can last a lifetime. Much sooner than you think, you can shape up, slim down, and look terrific!

DAY 1

Warm up
The pep up

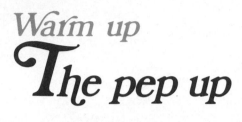

Starting position

Assume starting position.

a Jump up and switch foot and arm positions, bringing the right foot and right arm forward, the left foot and left arm back. Jump up again, returning arms and feet to starting position. Repeat 25 times.

a

Starting position

Warm up
The runner

a

b

Assume starting position.

a Lift the knees in an easy run-in-place for 50 counts. Swing the arms naturally as you run.

b With both hands, pull the right knee up toward the chest. Hold for 5 counts, while slowly pressing the nose toward the knee. Lower the leg to the floor. Repeat 3 times with each leg.

Starting position

Work that body

Assume starting position.

a Lift the left knee as high as possible. At the same time, press the arms straight forward, palms facing front. Return to starting position. Repeat 10 times with each leg.

a

Starting position

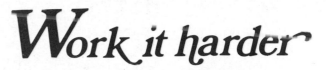

a

Assume starting position.

a Lift the left leg as high as possible. Keep the right foot flat on the floor. At the same time, press the arms forward, palms facing front. Return to starting position. Repeat 10 times with each leg.

b Stand with the feet wide apart, hands on the knees, head down. Round the back up as high as possible.

c Then flatten the back. Round and flatten the back 5 times.

b

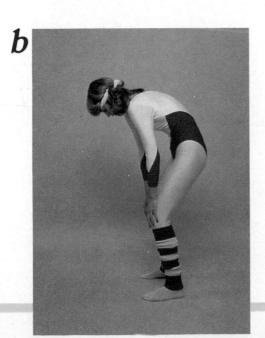

c

11

Quick kick

Starting position

Assume starting position.

a Kick the right leg up. Keep the left foot and both hands on the floor. Return to starting position. Repeat 15 times with each leg.

b Slide the heels forward, keeping the knees slightly bent. Place the hands behind the neck. Pull the head down toward the knees. Hold for 5 counts. Relax. Repeat 3 times.

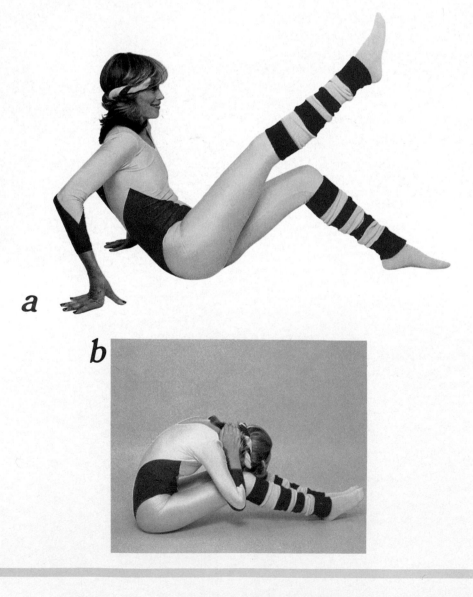

a

b

The compressor

Starting position

a

b

c

Assume starting position.

a Kick the right leg up. Bring the knee in toward the chest. Then kick straight forward. Return the knee to the chest. Kick up then forward 15 times with each leg.

b Fold the arms across the chest, hands gripping the arms near the shoulders. Slowly uncurl the back down to the floor. Keep the knees bent, feet on the floor.

c Grip the right knee with both hands and pull up to a sitting position. Always use the bent knee to help you sit up when doing this exercise. Uncurl down to the floor and sit up 5 times.

𝒯ummy tightener

Starting position

a

b

Assume starting position.

a Keep the head up off the floor during this exercise, to avoid jerking the neck when sitting up. Kick the right leg straight forward and sit up. Reach both hands toward the right ankle. Return to starting position. Repeat 10 times with each leg. (If your back is weak, grip the knee to help you sit up. Then kick forward and reach toward the ankle.)

b Sit with the feet flat on the floor. Pull the left knee up with both hands. Try to touch the nose to the knee. Hold for 5 counts. Do once with each knee.

The relaxer I

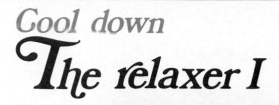

Starting position

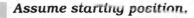

Assume starting position.

_a_ Lower the left leg to the floor.

_b_ Bend the left knee in toward the chest. Then extend the leg back up to the starting position. Repeat 10 times with each leg.

a

b

Assume starting position.

_a_ Round the back, pressing it down toward the floor. Slowly lower both legs to the floor. Keep the feet flat.

_b_ Bend the knees in toward the chest. Then extend the legs back up to the starting position. Repeat 10 times.

The relaxer II

Starting position

a

b

DAY 2

The invigorator

Starting position

b

a

Assume starting position.

a Jump up and cross the right foot to the floor in front of the left. At the same time, cross the arms in front of the chest. Keep the arms straight. Jump to return to starting position.

b Jump up and cross the right foot to the floor behind the left. Cross the arms in front again. Jump to return to starting position. Repeat 20 times.

16

Starting position

Assume starting position.

a Lift the knees in an easy run-in-place. While constantly running, move the arms as follows: Bend the elbows in toward the body. Then extend the arms straight forward.

b Bend the elbows in and extend the arms straight up. Then bend the elbows in and extend the arms forward again.

c Now bend the elbows in and extend the arms out to the sides. Keep running until you repeat the arm movement (bend, forward, bend, up, bend, forward, bend, side) 20 times.

a

Warm up
The vitalizer

b

c

Starting position

Assume starting position.

a Keep the hands on the elbows. Move the arms strongly to the left side. Then move the arms to the right side. Repeat 25 times.

b Place the hands on the waist. Slowly turn the torso to the left. Then turn to the right. Turn the torso smoothly. Do not jerk or turn beyond the normal range. Repeat 10 times.

Waistline whittler

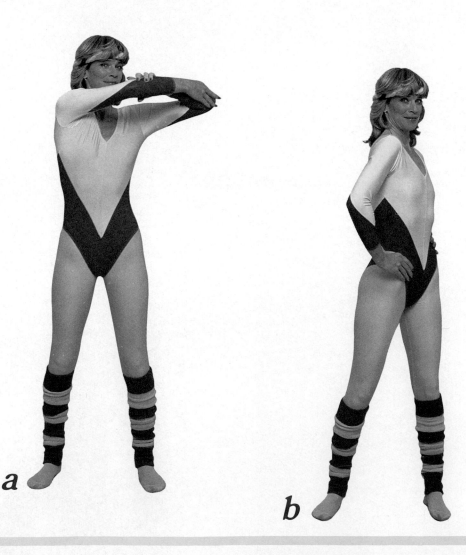

a

b

Starting position

Keep whittling

a

Assume starting position.

a Lift the left leg up to the side. At the same time, press the arms to the left. Keep the hands on the elbows. Lower the leg and return the arms to the center. Repeat 10 times with each leg.

b Place the hands on the waist. Slowly pull the elbows forward. Then press the elbows back. Repeat 5 times.

b

The firmer

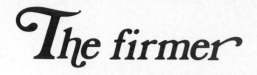

Assume starting position.

a Kick the right leg up. Then bend the knee in toward the chest.

b Kick the right leg out to the side. Return the knee to the chest. Kick up then to the side 10 times with each leg.

Starting position

a

b

Assume starting position.

_a_ Kick the right leg up as high as possible.

_b_ Bend the right leg, turning the knee to the side and down to the floor. Repeat 10 times with each leg.

Starting position

The turnout

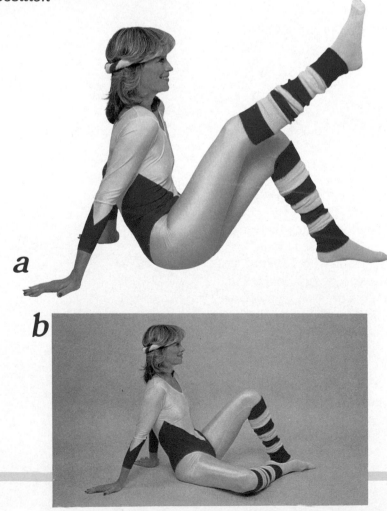

_a_

_b_

Tighten up

Starting position

a

b

Assume starting position.

a Keep the head off the floor during this exercise, to avoid jerking the neck when sitting up. Kick the right leg up and sit up. Reach both hands toward the right ankle. Return to starting position. Repeat 10 times with each leg. (If your back is weak, grip the knee to help you sit up. Then kick up and reach toward the ankle.)

b Now place the head on the floor. Lift the hips, pressing down on the arms. Hold for 5 counts. Lower the hips to the floor. Repeat 3 times.

Cool down
Get your kicks

Starting position

a

*a*With the back on the floor, kick the left leg then the right leg straight up 4 times. Then sit up and kick each leg straight forward 4 times. Kick up and forward 10 times. (If your back is weak, do not sit up. Kick up and forward keeping the back on the floor.)

*b*Extend the legs forward, feet turned out, hands on the floor. Lift the hips off the floor in a long stretch. Hold for 5 counts. Lower the hips to the floor. Repeat 3 times.

b

Starting position

Cool down
Pendulum pull

a

b

Assume starting position.

*a*Lower the legs forward slightly (about one-fourth of the way down). Return legs to a straight up position.

*b*Then press the legs back toward the head. Return to straight up position. Repeat 10 times. (For back support in this exercise, round the back, pressing it toward the floor. If it is more comfortable, place the hands under the hips for support.)

23

DAY 3

Starting position

Warm up
Movin'

Assume starting position.

a Lift and lower both heels, coming up and down on the toes. Keep the knees slightly bent. At the same time, swing the forearms forward and back. Repeat 25 times.

b Shake both arms and the right leg for 10 counts. Then shake the arms and the left leg for 10 counts.

a

b

Starting position

Movin' on

Assume starting position.

a Hop on the right foot and lift the left knee. At the same time, bring the right elbow down to touch the knee. Keep the right hand on the back of the neck. Return to starting position. Repeat 10 times with each knee.

a

Assume starting position.

a Lift the left knee up to the side, trying to reach waist height. At the same time, swing the right arm straight forward and up. Return the arm and the leg to starting position. Repeat 10 times with each knee.

b Place the arms at the sides. Slowly rotate both arms to turn the palms out to the sides. Then rotate to turn the palms in again. Repeat 5 times.

Rise and shine

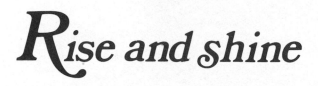

Starting position

a

b

a

Double lift

b

c

Assume starting position.

a Lift the left knee up to the side, swinging the right arm forward and up. Return the arm and leg to starting position.

b Now lift the left leg straight up to the side, swinging the right arm up again. Return to starting position. Repeat, lifting the knee then the leg, 10 times with each leg.

c Lower the head and round the back so that the chest is over the floor. Keep the knees slightly bent. Slowly swing the arms side to side 10 times.

Inch subtracter

Starting position

Assume starting position.

a Kick the left leg up as high as possible. At the same time, extend the arms up toward the foot.

b Bend the knee in and kick out to the left side, swinging both arms to the right side. Kick up then to the side 10 times with each leg. (If you feel discomfort in the small of the back, stop to rest briefly. Then continue the exercise.)

a

b

Starting position

Circle sensation

a

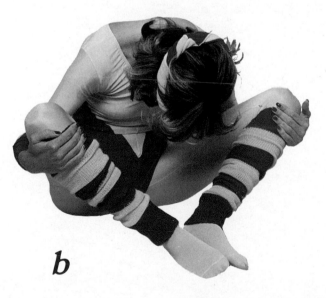

b

Assume starting position.

a Move the arms in a large circle above the knees, 10 times clockwise, 10 times counterclockwise. Keep the feet off the floor. (If this is difficult at first, do the exercise with the feet on the floor until you build up strength.)

b Now place the feet on the floor. Grasp the knees and pull them out to the sides. At the same time, pull the head and shoulders down. Hold for 5 counts. Relax. Repeat 3 times.

Starting position

Assume starting position.

a Supporting the weight on the hands and the heels, lift the hips off the floor. Keep the legs straight.

b Lift the left leg straight up. Hold for 3 counts. Lower the leg to the floor. Keeping the hips off the floor, repeat 5 times with each leg. Bending the elbows, lower the hips to the floor. Repeat the sequence 3 times.

c Sit with the legs extended, arms at the sides. Raise the shoulders as high as possible. Lower shoulders. Repeat 3 times.

a

The complete feat

b

c

Cool down
The lengthener

Starting position

Assume starting position.

a Lower the left arm and left leg. At the same time, touch the right hand to the back of the right leg. Then reverse arm and leg positions, lowering the right arm and leg, touching the left hand to the left leg. Repeat, swinging arms and legs up and down, 15 times. (Do this exercise keeping the head slightly off the floor or on the floor, whichever feels better for your back.)

a

Starting position

Cool down
Side slimmer

a

b

Assume starting position.

a Lower the left leg to the floor to the left side. Return leg to starting position. Repeat 5 times with each leg.

b Place the legs forward on the floor, knees slightly bent. Place the hands on the floor, fingers pointing back. Lean the torso forward, head down. Hold for 5 counts. Then return to starting position. Repeat the entire exercise 3 times.

31

DAY 4

Starting position

Warm up
Keep movin'

Assume starting position.

a Hop on the left foot, moving in a large circle. Then hop around this imaginary circle on the right foot. Repeat 5 times on each leg.

a

Starting position

Warm up
Keep movin' on

Assume starting position.

a Hop on the right foot, lifting the left leg straight up. At the same time, bring the right elbow down to touch the left knee. Keep the right hand on the back of the neck. Return to starting position. Repeat 5 times with each leg. Work up to 10 times with each leg.

b Stand with the feet apart, knees bent, hands on the knees. Raise the shoulders as high as possible. Hold for 5 counts. Lower shoulders. Repeat 3 times.

a

b

Starting position

The kicker

Assume starting position.

a Lift the left leg straight up, touching the left ankle with both hands. Lower the arms and the leg. Repeat 10 times with each leg.

a

Starting position

The rewarder

Assume starting position.

*a*Lift the left knee, crossing it toward the right side. At the same time, swing both arms down to the left. Return to starting position.

*b*Now lift the left leg up to the left side. At the same time, swing both arms straight down toward the right leg. Return to starting position. Repeat, lifting the knee then the leg, 10 times with each leg.

a

b

The tilt

Starting position

a

b

Assume starting position.

a Keeping the left knee bent back, lift the right leg as high as possible. Lower the leg to the floor. Repeat 10 times. Then reverse leg positions and lift the left leg 10 times.

b Return to starting position. Supporting the weight on the right hand and left knee, lift the hips as high as possible. At the same time, extend the left arm up in a long stretch. Hold for 5 counts. Return to starting position. Repeat 3 times on each side.

Starting position

Cross-touch shaper

a

Assume starting position.

a Lift the right leg up as high as possible. At the same time, touch the left hand to the right foot. Return to starting position. Repeat 10 times. Then reverse leg positions and lift the left leg 10 times.

*L*ift-off

Starting position

Assume starting position.

a Keeping the hips off the floor, lift the right leg straight up. Hold for 3 counts.

b Then lower the right leg to the floor at the side. Lift the leg straight up again. Then lower the leg forward to starting position. Repeat 5 times with each leg.

c Sit with the legs forward, arms out to the sides, palms up. Rotate the arms all the way around until the palms are turned up again in back. Hold for 5 counts. Then return to starting position. Repeat the entire exercise 3 times.

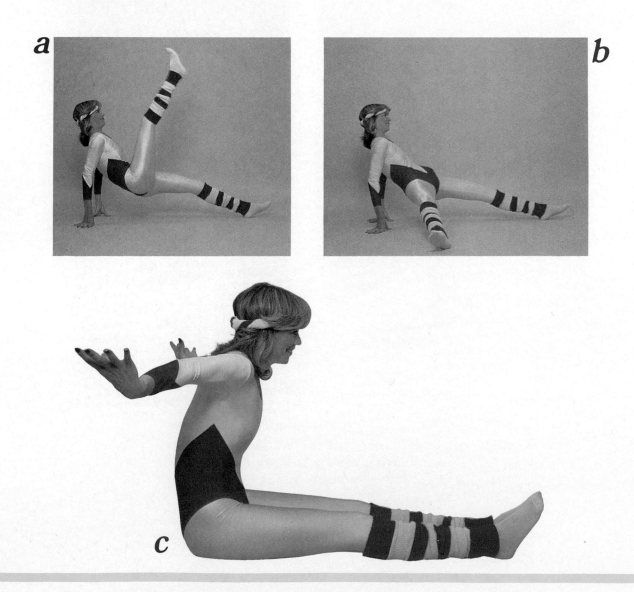

a

b

c

Cool down
Twist thin

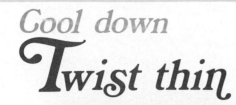

Starting position

Assume starting position.

a Lift the right leg and swing it across to the left. Touch the right foot with the left hand. Return to starting position. Then swing the left leg across to the right, touching the foot with the right hand. Return to starting position. Repeat 20 times.

a

Starting position

Cool down
The victory V

a

Assume starting position.

a Bend the knees up toward the chest, lifting the feet off the floor. Encircle the knees with the arms.

b Then extend the legs straight forward and slightly up. Swing the arms out to the sides. Keeping the feet off the floor, bring the knees in and extend the legs 5 times. Return to starting position and rest briefly. Then bring the knees in and extend the legs 5 more times.

b

DAY 5

Warm up
The fighter

Starting position

Assume starting position.

a Hop on the right foot, lifting the left knee as high as possible. At the same time, punch the right fist straight across to the left side. Return to starting position.

b Hop again, lifting the knee, and punch downward past the left hip. Return to starting position. Repeat 20 times on each side.

a

b

Warm up
Hop to it

Assume starting position.

a Holding the right foot in back, hop on the left foot 10 times.

b Holding the right foot in front, hop on the left foot 10 more times. Then hop on the right foot, 10 times holding the left foot in back, 10 times holding the foot in front.

Starting position

a

b

Starting position

a

Swing up

b

Assume starting position.

a Bending the left knee, bend the torso down to the left. Touch the right hand to the floor outside the left foot.

b Swing the torso and right arm up to the right, pivoting on the left foot. Touch the floor and swing up 10 times to each side.

The press

Starting position

a

Assume starting position.

a Very slowly press the hips forward as far as possible. Use only the muscles of the pelvic structure, not the back muscles, to tilt the hips forward. Hold for 5 counts. Return to starting position. Repeat 5 times. Rest briefly. Repeat 5 more times.

b Bend the knees lower, reaching the hands down toward the floor.

c Straightening the legs, swing the arms and torso up to the right side. Swing the arms and torso back down, bending the knees. Then swing up to the left side. Repeat 10 times.

b

c

Super circles

Starting position

a

b

Assume starting position.

a Lift the right leg and move it in a large circle 10 times. Reverse leg positions and circle the left leg 10 times.

b Place the hands on the floor for support. Lift the hips off the floor. Lift and lower the right leg 5 times. Reverse leg positions and repeat with the left leg 5 times.

Starting position

The trimmer

a

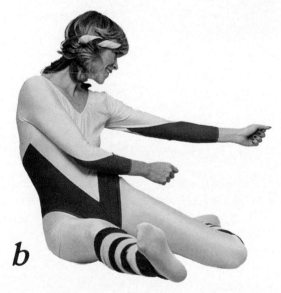

b

Assume starting position.

a Lift the right leg and swing it across to the left side. At the same time, swing the arms to the right.

b Then swing the leg across to the right side, swinging arms to the left. Swing the right leg and the arms back and forth 20 times without returning the right leg to the floor. Reverse leg positions and repeat 20 times with the left leg.

Starting position

Long lift

a

b

Assume starting position.

*a*With the left leg bent back, hold the ankle with the left hand. Lift the right leg straight up. Return the leg to the floor. Repeat 10 times. Reverse hand and leg positions and repeat 10 times with the left leg.

*b*Grasp the knees and pull them toward the chest. Raise the head and shoulders, pressing the head toward the knees. Hold for 5 counts. Lower the head and the feet to the floor. Repeat 5 times.

Cool down
Twist sit

Starting position

a Lift the head off the floor. Then sit up. Lower the left leg to the floor. Bend the right knee, turning it to the side on the floor. Swing the arms right, twisting the torso right. Do this all in one smooth movement. Return to starting position. Repeat 5 times to each side.

b Lie on the back, knees bent, hands behind the head. Roll the head and shoulders forward off the floor, keeping the back on the floor. Hold for 5 counts. Lower. Repeat 5 times.

a

b

Starting position

Cool down
The pull up

a

b

Assume starting position.

a Rounding the back slightly, tilt the hips back. Stay in this collapsed hip position for support.

b Very slowly lift the left leg straight up. Grasp the knee with both hands. Pull the leg toward you, pressing the head down toward the knee. Hold for 5 counts. Slowly lower the leg to the floor. Repeat 5 times with each leg.

DAY 6

Warm up
Side stretcher

Starting position

a

b

Assume starting position.

a Hop on the left foot, bending the right knee to bring the right foot up in front. Touch the left hand to the right foot. Return to starting position.

b Hop on the left foot again, crossing the right foot up in back, touching the foot with the left hand. Return to starting position. Repeat, crossing the foot in front then in back, 10 times with each leg.

Starting position

a

Warm up
High kicker

Assume starting position.

a Hop on the right foot, kicking the left leg straight up in front. Touch both hands to the left ankle. Return to starting position.

b Then kick the left leg up to the side. Swing both arms up to the sides. Return to starting position. Repeat, kicking forward then to the side, 5 times with the left leg, 5 times with the right. Then repeat 5 times left, 5 times right.

b

Assume starting position.

a Lunge to the left, bending the left knee. At the same time, swing the arms up and over to the left side. Hold for 5 counts. Return to starting position. Repeat 8 times to each side.

b Stand with the feet wide apart. Clasp the hands straight out in front of the body, palms turned out. Leaning the torso, press the hands to the right side, then to the left side. Repeat 10 times.

The lunge

Starting position

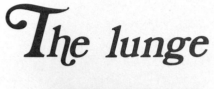

a

b

Pivot push

Starting position

a

Assume starting position.

a Pivoting on the left foot, turn the torso to the right. Bend the right knee and touch both hands to the knee. Return to starting position. Then pivot to the left, touching hands to the left knee. Return to starting position. Repeat 10 times.

b Stand with the torso bent forward. Alternately circle the arms forward, like swimming strokes. While continuing this swimming motion with the arms, move the arms and the torso to the right then to the left 8 times.

b

Around the world

Starting position

Assume starting position.

a Extend both legs out to the right side. Bend the knees in to the starting position. Then extend the legs out to the left side. Return to starting position. Repeat, extending the legs right then left, 10 times.

b From the starting position, kick both legs up. Bend the knees in again.

c Then kick the legs forward, swinging the arms out to the sides. Return arms and legs to starting position. Repeat, kicking up then forward, 5 times.

a

b

c

Super lifts I

Starting position

Assume starting position.

aLift both legs up from the side as high as possible. Touch the feet with the left hand. Lower the legs to the side to return to starting position. Lift and lower the legs 5 times from the right side, 5 times from the left side. Work up to 10 times from each side.

bIn the starting position, reach the left hand toward the left ankle.

c Swing the left arm and the legs up and over to the floor on the left side. Reach the right hand toward the right ankle. Then swing the legs back over to the right side. Repeat 6 times.

Starting position

a

*S*uper lifts II

Assume starting position.

a Raise both legs straight up from the right side. Then lower the legs straight forward to the floor, keeping the weight on the right hip. Lift the legs straight up again. Then lower them to the side to return to starting position. Repeat 5 times from the right side, 5 times from the left side. Work up to 8 times from each side.

b Sit, hands on the floor, elbows bent. With weight on the hands and hips, extend both legs straight up. Lower the left leg to the floor on the left side, following with the right leg.

c Raise the right leg up, following with the left leg. Swing the legs over to the floor on the right side. Swing the legs up and over to the left side then the right side 10 times.

b

c

Starting position

Assume starting position.

a Rounding the back slightly, tilt the hips back to support the spine. Lift the left leg.

b Very slowly move the leg in a high arch up to the side, then down to the floor on the left side. Then arch the left leg up again to return it to the floor in front. Repeat 5 times with each leg.

Cool down
Feeling strong

a

b

Starting position

Cool down
Feeling stronger

Assume starting position.

a Rounding the back slightly, tilt the hips back to support the spine. Lift the left leg up to the left side as high as possible.

b Holding the left leg up to the side, lift the right leg off the floor. Hold both legs in that position for 5 counts. Lower both legs to starting position. Repeat the lift, then hold, 3 times to each side.

a

b

DAY 7

Starting position

The marionette

Assume starting position.

a Alternately raise the right heel then the left heel by lifting the hips. Keep the knees stiff. At the same time, alternately move the arms up and down. Repeat, lifting the right heel then the left heel, 30 times.

b Bend the knees to place the fingertips on the floor in front of the feet.

c Slowly straighten the legs until the knees are only slightly bent. Do not straighten completely. Hold for 5 counts. Then uncurl the back to return to an upright position.

a

b

c

Warm up
Get in action

Starting position

Assume starting position.

a Hop on the left foot, kicking the right leg across to the left. At the same time, swing both arms to the right. Return to starting position. Repeat 10 times with each leg.

b Clasp the elbows above the head. Lower the head forward and press the arms back. Hold for 5 counts. Relax. Repeat 3 times.

a

b

Starting position

The deflator

a

b

Assume starting position.

a Bend the knees and lower the hips straight down. At the same time, turn the torso to the left. Swing the arms down to touch the outside of the left ankle. Return to starting position. Repeat 10 times to each side.

b Clasp the hands to the elbows. Bend the knees and place the elbows on the knees. Slowly straighten the legs. Hold for 5 counts. Bend and straighten the legs 5 times.

***B**elt tightener*

Starting position

Assume starting position.

aKick both legs out to the left side. At the same time, swing both arms to the right. Bend the knees in toward the chest. Then kick the legs out to the right side, swinging the arms to the left. Bring the knees in. Repeat, kicking left then right, 10 times.

bExtend the right leg forward on the floor. Grasp the left knee with both hands. Slowly uncurl the back down to the floor.

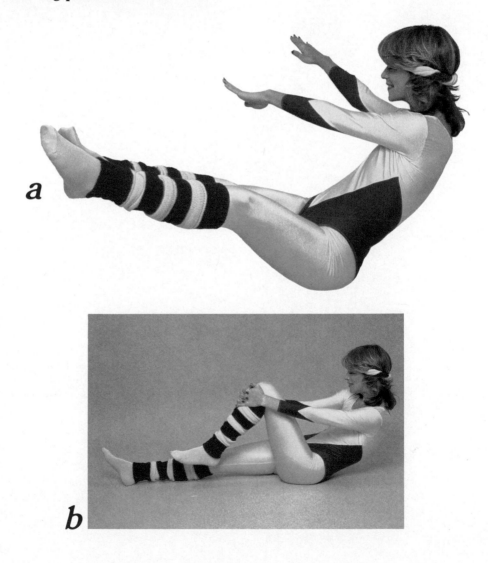

a

b

Circle cincher

Starting position

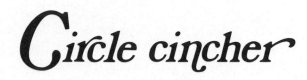

a

b

Assume starting position.

a Lift the left leg off the floor. Move the leg in large circles to the side. Circle each leg 15 times.

b Return to the starting position. Lift the left leg up from the side and lower it forward to the floor. Return the leg to the side. Repeat 15 times with each leg.

The scissors

Assume starting position.

a Lift the head off the floor, chin toward the chest. Raise the left arm and the right leg, sitting up to touch the hand to the ankle. Return to starting position. Then repeat with the right arm and the left leg. Return to starting position. Repeat 10 times. (To avoid jerking the neck, be sure to lift the head off the floor before sitting up.)

b Roll over onto the side. Pull the knees toward the chest, head toward the knees. Hold for 5 counts. Relax. Repeat 3 times.

Starting position

a

b

The extensor

Assume starting position.

a Lift the head off the floor to avoid jerking the neck. Then extend both legs straight up, sit up, and touch the hands to the ankles. Return to starting position. Repeat 10 times.

b Sit, hands on the floor, left knee bent with the foot on the floor, right leg extended forward. Lift the hips off the floor in a long stretch. Hold for 5 counts. Lower the hips to the floor. Reverse leg positions and repeat the stretch once more.

Starting position

a

b

Cool down
The strengthener

Starting position

a

Assume starting position.

a Extend the left arm forward. At the same time, extend the left leg back. Return to starting position. Repeat 10 times with the left arm and leg, 10 times with the right arm and leg.

b Place the hands and knees on the floor. Lift the hips. Slowly try to straighten the legs and press the heels back toward the floor. Hold for 5 counts. Uncurl the back to return to an upright position.

b

Starting position

The recycler

a

b

c

Assume starting position.

a Lift the knees in a loose, easy run-in-place for 30 counts. Swing the arms naturally as you run.

b Place the sole of the left foot against the right ankle, left toe on the floor. Bend the right knee slightly.

c Slowly bend, reaching for the ankles with both hands. Hold for 5 counts. Uncurl the back to return to an upright position. Reverse foot positions and repeat the stretch once.